Air Force Global Strike Command

STRATEGIC MASTER PLAN
2014

TABLE OF CONTENTS

FOREWORD

The nuclear mission demands a special trust and responsibility. Because Air Force Global Strike Command is entrusted with the nation's most powerful weapons, I would like to lay out the strategic environment in which we find ourselves, the challenges we must address, and the plan to do so. During the five years AFGSC has existed, the nuclear enterprise has been renewed, rekindled, reinvigorated, and strengthened. We will continue to build upon that effort; we will challenge ourselves to seek out and resolve any current weaknesses in the enterprise. Finally, we will prepare for the future by continuing to strengthen the nuclear enterprise and culture of compliance while modernizing both nuclear and conventional global strike capabilities.

As the Secretary of the Air Force and the Chief of Staff have said, Airmen see things globally – without boundaries. That is especially true of AFGSC Airmen, whose focus is inherently global and strategic. Our mission at AFGSC is vitally important. We provide the nation effective deterrence, and when called upon, rapid global strike.

To the men and women of AFGSC – officer, enlisted, civilian, active, Guard and Reserve – I'm proud of each and every one of you who bravely defends the nation and secures our freedom. Through your dedication and through your effort, I am confident we will be a model command in the United States Air Force and provide a strong and reliable deterrent force for America and our allies. I am extremely proud to be your commander. I promise to give you my best every day, and I count on you to do the same. I know that you will. I am excited about the future and look forward to the challenges ahead.

STEPHEN W. WILSON
Lieutenant General, USAF
Commander

Executive Summary

As long as nuclear weapons exist, the United States will maintain a safe, secure, and effective arsenal, both to deter potential adversaries and to assure US allies and other security partners.[1] The *2010 Nuclear Posture Review (NPR)* provides clear guidance for Air Force Global Strike Command (AFGSC) to provide forces for nuclear deterrence and global strike operations. This AFGSC Strategic Master Plan (SMP) details the future strategic environment, future challenges, command vision, values and priorities. Our vision and priorities underpin our values: responsibility, self-assessment, adherence, expertise, pride, respect, and safety. We will use these values to consolidate our recent gains across the nuclear enterprise and to complete the restoration of a culture that fully embraces the special trust and responsibility of nuclear weapons.

As a warfighting Component MAJCOM (C-MAJCOM) to United States Strategic Command (USSTRATCOM), AFGSC forces will execute assigned deterrence, assurance, and global strike missions. As a force provider, AFGSC will organize, train, and equip both conventional and nuclear combat forces for the President and combatant commanders (CCDRs). Intercontinental ballistic missile (ICBM) forces are currently deployed in a nuclear deterrent role, and AFGSC bombers plan and execute deterrence and Global Power/Strike operations to provide USSTRATCOM with a visible deterrent capability. AFGSC will continue to support these forces and missions and prepare to provide additional combat power as required to address challenges and threats to the United States.

The strategic environment continues to present a very dynamic and uncertain picture. The number of state and non-state actors that can produce strategic effects across the spectrum of conflict is growing in both quantity and complexity. As stated in the *2012 Defense Strategic Guidance (DSG)*, the US Armed Forces must maintain a safe, secure, and effective nuclear deterrent, deter and defeat aggression, project power despite anti-access/area denial (A2/AD) challenges, and counter weapons of mass destruction (WMD),[2] while assuring our allies and partners of our commitment to our cooperative security agreements. In current and future conflicts, AFGSC forces are required to survive and operate in threat environments ranging from low threat/permissive environments to highly contested A2/AD environments. To overcome these obstacles and fulfill our vision, AFGSC will engage with higher headquarters, political leadership, and defense industry leaders to recapitalize, maintain, and modernize the nuclear and global strike enterprise.

The AFGSC priorities are:

Priority 1. Deter and assure with a safe, secure, and effective nuclear force

Priority 2. Win the fight

Priority 3. Continue to strengthen and empower the team

Priority 4. Shape the future

These priorities provide the necessary direction to fulfill the Air Force's number one priority, to *"Continue to Strengthen the Air Force Nuclear Enterprise."*[3]

  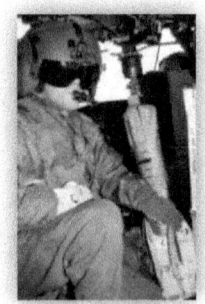

---

[1] *Nuclear Posture Review Report: April 2010.* Department of Defense, 6 April 2010, p. iii.
[2] *Sustaining U.S. Global Leadership: Priorities for 21st Century Defense.* Department of Defense, January 2012 (aka *2012 DSG), 4-6.*
[3] 2013 Air Force Priorities Presentation, AF/CCX, July 2013. Website:
   https://www.my.af.mil/gcss-af/USAF/AFP40/d/s6925EC1356510FB5E044080020E329A9/Files/editorial/Air Force Priorities.pdf

As AFGSC continues to mature and balance the nuclear deterrent and conventional global strike mission sets, competing requirements and limited resources create risk. Through prioritization, AFGSC will balance resources and risk to meet the objectives found in the *2013 DoD Strategic Choices and Management Review, 2013 USAF Posture Statement, 2012 DSG, 2014 Quadrennial Defense Review* (QDR) and the overall guidance contained in the *2010* NPR.

Our vision and mission statements clearly articulate the environment for a values-based culture where all members comprehend the special trust and responsibility associated with the nuclear enterprise. Our priorities align the AFGSC SMP with the *2013 USAF Posture Statement*, and the principles and missions found in the *2012 DSG*.

Section 1: Introduction

"As a significant portion of America's deterrent capability, Air Force global strike provides the Nation the ability to project military power more rapidly, more flexibly, and with a lighter footprint than other military options. The Air Force's nuclear deterrent and conventional precision strike forces can credibly deny adversary objectives or impose unacceptable costs by effectively holding any target on the planet at risk and, if necessary, disabling or destroying targets promptly, even from bases in the continental United States. Global strike may entail close support to troops at risk, interdicting enemy fielded forces, or striking an adversary's vital centers from great distances. Credible long-range strike capabilities are indispensable for deterrence and provide fundamental military capabilities to underpin U.S. military power."

- *USAF Posture Statement 2013*[4]

As a warfighting Component MAJCOM (C-MAJCOM) to United States Strategic Command (USSTRATCOM), AFGSC forces will execute assigned deterrence, assurance, and global strike missions. In addition, Air Force Global Strike Command (AFGSC) is charged to organize, train, and equip (OT&E) both nuclear and conventional combat forces for the President of the United States and combatant commanders (CCDRs). Specifically, AFGSC provides on-demand, agile combat power to CCDRs specializing in strategic nuclear deterrence and global strike operations.

Purpose

The 2014 AFGSC Strategic Master Plan (SMP) outlines the strategic vision and priorities for our command to move forward with presentation, employment, sustainment, and modernization of global strike capabilities. The AFGSC SMP is the primary means by which the Commander, Air Force Global Strike Command, communicates his strategic vision and priorities to the command to support the President and the CCDRs. The AFGSC SMP charts a course for mission accomplishment in a dynamic operating environment. The command priorities support the achievement of objectives outlined in the 2013 USAF Posture Statement, *2012 Defense Strategic Guidance (DSG), 2011 National Military Strategy* (NMS) and a variety of higher headquarters guidance documents, to include the *2014 Quadrennial Defense Review* (QDR) and *2010 Nuclear Posture Review* (NPR).

---

[4] *USAF Posture Statement: April 2013*. Department of the Air Force, April 2013, 13.

The AFGSC SMP also describes the current strategic environment and identifies future challenges. These challenges provide the necessary boundaries to ensure realistic solutions to complex problems, especially in light of demanding requirements and constrained resources. Given these challenges, the AFGSC SMP provides strategic guidance, the command's vision, and a mission statement to establish a clear understanding of the command's purpose and direction and aid in command goal development. The AFGSC strategic priorities originate from our vision and values. AFGSC command goals will align with the strategic priorities; they will be published separately and supported by subordinate goals. All AFGSC personnel, from our most senior commanders to our youngest airmen, should use this document and the command's priorities found herein as the foundation for their activities.

Command Overview

"In our nuclear inventory we have two-thirds of the triad that provides nuclear deterrence to the United States of America. That's a huge responsibility. ... It's a big deal for us. We can't afford to ever get this wrong."

- General Mark A. Welsh, Chief of Staff, USAF[5]

AFGSC Mission Statement

"Develop and provide combat ready forces for nuclear deterrence and global strike operations...
    -- Safe
        -- Secure
            -- Effective
                to support the President of the United States and Combatant Commanders."

Our mission rests upon individual responsibility, superior technical expertise, critical self-assessment, uncompromising adherence to directives, and respect for the worth and dignity of every Airman in the command. AFGSC's strategic deterrence and global strike role is a critical mission that supports national objectives and the Air Force's mission to *"fly, fight, and win...*in air, space, and cyberspace."

The AFGSC Vision

American Airmen with special trust and responsibility for the most powerful weapons in our Nation's arsenal... an elite, highly disciplined team... a model command.

AFGSC Commander's Intent

Continue to strengthen the nuclear enterprise while modernizing both nuclear and conventional global strike capabilities. To accomplish our mission, we must keep in mind four priorities:
    1. Deter our adversaries and assure our allies with a safe, secure, and effective nuclear deterrent;
    2. Win the current fight around the globe;
    3. Continue to strengthen and empower the team to accomplish the mission;
    4. Shape the future by providing modern nuclear and conventional global strike capabilities to the President and the combatant commanders.

The disciplined execution of current operations in support of USSTRATCOM and the CCDRs and the ongoing effort to establish a culture that embraces the special trust and responsibility of nuclear weapons are critical for the success of AFGSC. AFGSC will provide highly disciplined Airmen, in both nuclear and conventional mission sets, to the President and CCDRs. To enable this objective, AFGSC will support deliberate efforts to develop professional Airmen, promote resiliency, and strengthen expertise in nuclear and conventional global strike operations. We will accomplish this by instilling a culture that is both strictly compliant and appropriately innovative. Following our leaders and procedures to the letter is the very fabric of nuclear operations. At the same time, frank self-assessment, innovation, and systemic improvement are indispensable to developing our people and improving our quality of life, and will provide the efficiencies to sustain our efforts to complete our exacting mission.

AFGSC must continue to sustain and modernize assigned weapons systems and support infrastructure to ensure there is a viable and visible deterrent and global strike capability well into the future. These efforts are crucial components of AFGSC's ability to ensure strategic stability, deter the nation's adversaries, and assure US allies and partners.

---

[5] Gen Mark A. Welsh, Chief of Staff, US Air Force. Address. Air Force Association Air & Space Conference and Technology Exposition, Washington, DC, 18 September 2012.

Command Values

Individual responsibility, self-assessment, adherence, expertise, pride, respect, safety, resilience, and innovation are characteristic values of AFGSC. Taken together, these values will focus the actions of each individual to ensure that AFGSC upholds the Air Force core values of *"Integrity first, service before self, and excellence in all we do."* As individuals, we must internalize and exemplify these values. As a team, we will expect them of each other to enable our confidence and cohesion. As a command, we recognize their fundamental importance and will ensure we uphold these standards consistently and fairly.

AFGSC values are:

1. *Individual responsibility for mission success*
    Our work is a team effort, but that work depends on each individual—from the commander to the newest Airman—doing his or her part by performing in a broad range of challenging environments. Every action contributes to the command's success.

2. *Critical self-assessment of our performance*
    "...to establish and sustain an uncompromising standard of excellence in nuclear operations. This will require hands-on leadership, at all levels, to instill a strong culture of compliance that internalizes precision, reliability, and critical self-assessment."[6]

3. *Uncompromising adherence to directives*
    The Commander's intent for this value can only be met by adopting a culture where strict compliance is the standard.

4. *Superior technical and weapons system expertise*
    "The mission of safeguarding our vital nuclear capabilities and maintaining our nuclear deterrence mission requires the sharpest focus on excellence and unwavering adherence to precision and reliability. One might even say that, in the business of nuclear weapons, there 'is no room for error.'" [7]

5. *Persistent innovation at all levels*
    AFGSC will continue to further the Air Force legacy of innovation, position the command to take full advantage of opportunities to improve, and enable innovations that secure tomorrow's future.

6. *Pride in our nuclear heritage and mission*
    "...from heritage and experience, we expect [Air Force] Global Strike Command to carry forward a renewed commitment to the highest standards of professionalism, excellence, and nuclear expertise to guide the new generation of Airmen overseeing our nation's most critical military mission."[8]

7. *Respect for the worth and dignity of every Airman*
    AFGSC is committed to ensuring our people are afforded the respect and developmental opportunities they deserve.

8. *Safety in all things large...and small*
    Safety is everyone's responsibility, on and off duty, and fundamental to our mission. AFGSC has a special trust and responsibility for the most powerful weapons in our nation's arsenal and part of that responsibility is to keep our most critical asset, our people, safe and mission ready.[9]

These command values guide our Airmen through the many challenges of operating within the unique environment of Air Force Global Strike Command.

---

[6] Michael B. Donley, Secretary of the Air Force. Address. AFGSC activation ceremony, Barksdale AFB LA, 7 August 2009.
[7] Gen Norton A. Schwartz, Chief of Staff, US Air Force. Address. AFGSC activation ceremony, Barksdale AFB LA, 7 August 2009.
[8] Donley, Address, 7 August 2009.
[9] Lt Gen James M. Kowalski, *Critical Days of Summer* Memo to AFGSC Personnel, 24 May 2011.

Organizational Structure

Air Force Global Strike Command is charged to provide combat forces for nuclear deterrence and global strike operations to the President and the CCDRs. AFGSC is comprised of two Numbered Air Forces—the Eighth and the Twentieth—and maintains five Air Force bases. There are over 25,000 personnel in the command who operate, maintain, and support 450 intercontinental ballistic missiles (ICBMs), 24 UH-1N helicopters and 96 long-range, nuclear-capable bombers. Figure 1 is a graphic depiction of the units and forces that belong to or support AFGSC. The Air National Guard and Air Force Reserve units that support the command as part of the Air Force's Total Force Enterprise (TFE) are also found in Figure 1.

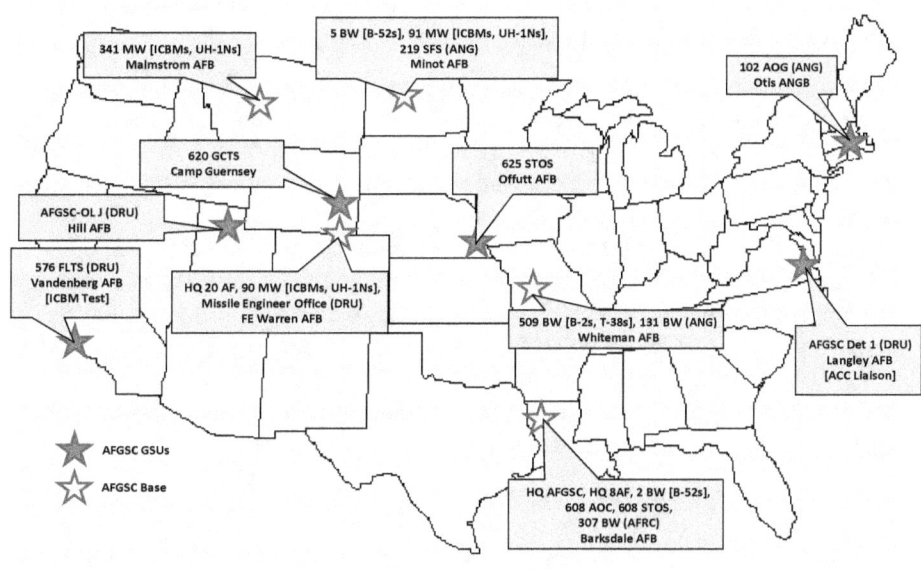

Figure 1. AFGSC Unit Locations

Section 2: Strategic Environment

"Our strategic and operational environment requires a deep understanding of our adversaries and potential adversaries in the context of our complex and interconnected operating space."

- Admiral Cecil D. Haney, Commander, United States Strategic Command[10]

Overview

The twenty-first century strategic environment continues to present a very dynamic and uncertain picture. The era in which the United States can project global military power virtually uncontested will likely end by 2030, if not before.[11] The potential state and non-state actors that can threaten the United States and its allies across the spectrum of conflict are growing in number and increasing in complexity.

Countries with geopolitical, military, and economic power or reach are becoming more prevalent and diverse, thus requiring a greater effort by the United States to work with key allies and partners to maintain stability and peace around the globe. Further exacerbating this situation are the influence of non-state actors (e.g., terrorists, insurgents, computer hackers), the proliferation of weapons of mass destruction (WMD) and their delivery means (e.g., ballistic missiles), and technological innovations which decrease the effectiveness of our current capabilities. As outlined in the *2011 Air Force Strategic Environmental Assessment* (AFSEA), potential adversaries (to include non-state actors) are developing the means to challenge US military power overseas and continue to look for ways to threaten the US homeland.[12] The relative rise of new powers, especially in the Asia-Pacific region, requires a strategic shift to that part of the globe for renewed focus and a rebalancing of US forces to meet the growing anti-access/area denial (A2/AD) challenges posed by those powers over the next 20 years.[13] In focusing a credible military force on the Asia-Pacific region, the United States will ensure free trade[14], assure our friends and allies, promote regional stability, and deter regional aggression.

Globalization enables the proliferation of technology, which continues to enhance the abilities of both state and non-state actors to challenge US military power. Adversaries continue to undermine international support for the United States, hamper domestic US resolve, and aim to damage the US economy by exploiting US vulnerabilities through asymmetric engagement in air, space, and cyberspace.[15] Adversaries also aim to develop the means to deny, degrade, disrupt, deceive, and destroy US military capabilities around the globe. More technologically advanced adversaries will employ anti-access strategies aimed at denying US forces access to the theater of operations. Where they cannot deny access, they will seek to deny the US freedom of action within the theater.

AFGSC-assigned forces are key components of the Department of Defense's (DoD's) means to defend and advance the United States' national interests. We must balance resources and risks to protect the key priorities in the 2014 QDR.[16] Fallout from the FY13 sequestration on resources in FY14 and beyond is still being assessed. While mitigation actions helped alleviate the most problematic and immediate FY13 funding shortfalls, the decisions we have been forced to make in short-term spending may increase total costs over the long run. The national fiscal situation drives uncertainty in the DoD budget.[17] Therefore, we must diligently advocate for appropriate capabilities, be thoughtful in requirements development, and be respectful of current and future resource constraints in execution and future year planning.[18]

---

[10] *ADM Cecil D. Haney "Combatant Commander's Guidance Memo #1,"* Headquarters United States Strategic Command, 27 November 2013, 1.

[11] *USAF Strategic Planning 2010-2030, Strategic Environmental Assessment.* Headquarters Air Force, 11 March 2011, 11.

[12] Ibid.

[13] *2012 DSG*, 2.

[14] Estimated at $1.3 trillion annually, U.S. Census Bureau, https://www.census.gov/foreign-trade/balance/c0016.html#2013

[15] *2011 AFSEA*, 11.

[16] 2014 QDR, 32.

[17] *USAF Posture Statement 2013*, 3-4.

[18] *Haney*, CCDR Guidance Memo, 2.

Strategic Threats

Nations with WMD and advanced conventional capabilities will continue to be potential strategic threats. Foreign intelligence and security services will continue efforts to gather information on US capabilities through human intelligence, signals intelligence, and imagery intelligence to replicate or mitigate US military advantages. Violent extremists and terrorist groups will continue to develop indirect means to strike the United States through recruitment and subversion of dissidents or through covert insertion. They will continue to pursue their goal of acquiring nuclear weapons and other WMD.[19]

Status of Threats, Short-Term (2014-2019)

Our potential adversaries continue to improve their military capabilities through the procurement and fielding of new fighters, radars, surface-to-air missiles (SAMs), and quieter ballistic missile and attack submarines. Upgrades to SAM systems will enhance anti-access within potential adversary layered defenses, challenging the United States' access to the theater of operations. Along with newer fighters, nations seek advanced air-to-air missiles with increased capabilities far beyond visual range engagements. The proliferation of WMD continues, with many nations seeing these capabilities as asymmetric means to counter the greater military capabilities of neighboring states.

Missile proliferation is progressing rapidly, with some nations reverse engineering and enhancing mature capabilities. Ballistic missile systems are no longer only a tactical threat as nations' research and development efforts reach for Intermediate Range Ballistic Missile (IRBM) and ICBM capabilities. Due to the WMD desires of many third world countries and the fast-paced development of ballistic missile and cruise missile technology, protection of the US Homeland and our allies will become more critical. Potential adversaries are also nearing initial operational capability for new ICBM, sea-launched ballistic missile capabilities, and land-attack cruise missiles. Along with new missile capabilities, adversaries will continue to exploit information operations by fielding enhanced electronic attack platforms while continuing to use media and cyber capabilities.

Status of Threats, Mid-Term (2020-2024)

Potential adversaries are designing and/or have developmental test beds for their fifth generation fighters and SAMs. Although some initial operational fielding could occur in the short-term, the quantities needed to be viable threats will not occur until the mid-term. The next generation of air-to-air missiles is expected to be fielded in the mid-term. The continued development of fifth generation SAM systems (e.g., S-500) will significantly enhance anti-access within adversary layered defenses. The fielding of a new generation of anti-satellite (ASAT) weapon capabilities will increase the risk to our nation's space based assets and when coupled with the S-500 battle management capability could create a formidable anti-access capability. The proliferation of fifth generation fighters and SAMs, as well as advanced radar capabilities and advanced missile accuracies, will transform current contested access environments into anti-access environments and challenge the advantage of low observable weapons and weapon systems.

Status of Threats, Far-Term (2025-Beyond)

Fifth generation aircraft, advanced radars, and SAMs will continue to proliferate. Potential adversaries will advance their ASAT capabilities to the point of holding any space-based asset at risk. Many nations will have developed their own space-based remote sensing capability, thus reducing US information dominance. In essence, the trends identified within the mid-term will continue with increased proliferation to other nation states. Coupled with the near-, mid-, and far-term threats, there are additional challenges that we face.

---

[19] NPR Report, 3.

Challenges

The challenges and responsibilities facing AFGSC are consistent with those described by the *2012 DSG*, which reminds us that "the United States will continue to lead global efforts with capable allies and partners to assure access to and use of the global commons, both by strengthening international norms of responsible behavior and by maintaining relevant and interoperable military capabilities."[20] Even so, the *2013 USAF Posture Statement* states, "the fiscal environment requires us to make trades between force structure, readiness, and modernization among the core missions to ensure the highest quality and ready Air Force possible."[21]

Most Likely Future Environment:
- Fiscally constrained operating environment due to economic pressures. Budgetary resources will decline; operational costs will constrain sustainment, modernization, recapitalization, and readiness
- Legacy force capabilities continue to erode in contested environments with continued adversary development and exportation of advanced air defense technologies, forcing key trades and priorities in our modernization, with the target being development of a smaller but more lethal force at high readiness
- Other nuclear armed states modernize and expand capabilities. Some non-state actors may seek to develop WMD as an asymmetric counter to overwhelming conventional power
- Consequently, to align with the DSG, AFGSC must continue to support the Air Force posture of improving the quality of our force by maintaining the agility, flexibility, and readiness to engage a full range of contingencies and threats[22]

Most Dangerous Future Environment:
- Non-state actors develop and/or employ nuclear devices as an asymmetric counter to overwhelming conventional power
- Fiscally restrained operating environment due to economic pressures. Budgetary resources decline; operational costs restrain sustainment, modernization, recapitalization, and readiness preventing necessary upgrades and creating a "hollow force," incapable of defending the Nation
- Lack of sustainment and modernization allow regional powers to successfully employ comprehensive A2/AD strategies, thereby further restraining the use of US diplomatic, informational, economic, and military instruments of power
- Consequently, as US freedom of action is limited, credibility of US extended deterrence declines, resulting in proliferation, regional arms races, and greater chance for conflict

---

[20] 2012 DSG, 3.
[21] *USAF Posture Statement 2013*, 3.
[22] *USAF Posture Statement 2013*, 2.

Section 3: Strategic Priorities and The Way Ahead

"The United States is going to remain … strongly committed to maintaining a capable and effective, safe, nuclear deterrent … We're going to invest in the modernization that we need to invest in to keep that deterrent stronger than it's ever been."

- Chuck Hagel, United States Secretary of Defense[23]

Strategic Priorities

AFGSC is responsible to USSTRATCOM as its air component to provide the ability to employ nuclear and conventional global strike air forces in support of US national objectives. As a force provider, AFGSC is responsible to organize, train, and equip forces to support CCDRs in performing nuclear and conventional deterrence and global strike operations. In each role, air component and force provider, AFGSC aligns its priorities with those of the Air Force[24], which provide the direction for the Air Force in support of national and joint objectives. The command's strategic priorities enable AFGSC to focus its efforts efficiently and effectively, providing important and unique contributions to the security of the nation and its allies.

Priority 1. Deter and assure with a safe, secure, and effective nuclear force

The 2014 QDR underscored the critical importance of the nuclear mission by stating, "Our nuclear deterrent is the ultimate protection against a nuclear attack on the United States, and through extended deterrence, it also serves to reassure our distant allies of their security against regional aggression. It also supports our ability to project power by communicating to potential nuclear-armed adversaries that they cannot escalate their way out of failed conventional aggression."[25] We understand the special trust and responsibility placed upon us by the Commander in Chief and the nation. Every day, with every Global Power bomber sortie, nuclear weapon system evaluation program (WSEP) mission, and ICBM Follow-on Operational Test & Evaluation ("Glory Trip"), we send a single consistent message - we stand ready to deter our foes, assure our friends and allies, and ensure a credible nuclear deterrent. In so doing, we support USSTRATCOM's top priority: *"Deter nuclear attack with a safe, secure, effective nuclear deterrent force."[26]*

Priority 2. Win the fight

AFGSC is responsible for providing combat forces for two legs of the strategic deterrent triad. The long-range bomber fleet and persistent ICBM force provide a comprehensive deterrent capability unmatched in the world. AFGSC forces must stand ready in their daily deterrent role while maintaining capability and readiness to support USSTRATCOM and the combatant commands when tasked. ICBMs are currently deployed in a nuclear deterrent role, and AFGSC bombers plan and execute deterrence and Global Power/Strike operations to provide USSTRATCOM with a visible deterrent capability. AFGSC bombers also support PACOM deterrence missions through participation in Continuous Bomber Presence (CBP), contributing to security and stability of that region.

Priority 3. Continue to strengthen and empower the team

As we move further into the twenty-first century, we will continue to strengthen the nuclear enterprise by looking at AFGSC systemically and critically. As a learning organization, we must build upon our shared vision of a model command made up of American Airmen with a special trust and responsibility. While honoring our heritage, we must not be mired in the past. We must challenge our assumptions of AFGSC culture, keeping the best and improving the rest. We must create a "culture of compliance" to all directives across AFGSC. The keys to creating this culture are standardization of processes, leadership accountability at all levels, and internalization of Air Force and AFGSC values. We will provide a safe, respectful, and productive work environment for every member of AFGSC. Likewise, AFGSC will strive to attract, develop, and retain a talented and diverse total force. Providing a positive work environment, recognizing the value of each individual, and enabling personal and

---

[23] Hagel, Chuck, Secretary of Defense. Address. F.E. Warren AFB, 9 January 2014.
[24] 2013 Air Force Priorities Presentation.
[25] *Quadrennial Defense Review Report 2014.* Department of Defense, 4 March 2014, 13.
[26] *Haney*, CCDR Guidance Memo, 2.

professional growth will provide a unified, resilient, and adaptable team enabled to accomplish AFGSC's mission of strategic deterrence.

Priority 4. Shape the future

AFGSC recognizes the responsibility to be efficient and effective stewards of resources in a fiscally constrained environment. We must be innovative, efficient, and effective in order to sustain and enhance our current force to meet tomorrow's challenges. The synergies achieved by upgrading AFGSC's nuclear and conventional capabilities support the Air-Sea Battle Concept (ASB), which describes what is necessary for the joint force to sufficiently shape the A2/AD environments to enable concurrent or follow-on power projection.[27] AFGSC will maintain and improve its ability to employ nuclear weapons in a range of scenarios, to include integration with conventional operations, and thereby maximize regional and overall deterrence and assurance. AFGSC will continue to advocate for development and funding of system sustainment and modernization to provide a credible, flexible, affordable, and adaptable deterrent for the President and the CCDRs. As the Core Function Lead (CFL) for Nuclear Deterrence Operations (NDO), AFGSC will partner with other agencies to manage the entire portfolio of AF nuclear assets. The current state of AFGSC-owned weapons/weapon systems and modernization efforts follow:

The Way Ahead

Bomber – B-52H Stratofortress - The B-52 is a venerable long-range heavy bomber with an impressive combat history spanning the Vietnam War and Operations DESERT STORM, ALLIED FORCE, ENDURING FREEDOM, and IRAQI FREEDOM. For more than 50 years, B-52 Stratofortresses have been the backbone of the manned strategic bomber force, performing strategic attack, close air support, air interdiction, offensive counter-air, and maritime global strike operations. It can carry a wide variety of conventional and nuclear bombs, missiles, and mines, and offers an unmatched capability to deliver long-range stand-off weapons, contributing to the AFGSC deterrence and assurance missions. To keep the B-52 viable until at least 2040, AFGSC is modernizing a number of critical capabilities. To keep pace with twenty-first century standards, AFGSC is upgrading the communication capability and crew interface through the Combat Network Communications Technology (CONECT) program, which is also an enabler for the Extremely High Frequency (EHF) communications network. Another funded upgrade is the 1760 Internal Weapons Bay Upgrade (IWBU), a modification allowing the B-52 to carry the Joint Direct Attack Munition (JDAM), Joint Air-to-Surface Standoff Missile (JASSM), JASSM-ER (Extended Range) and Miniature Air Launched Decoy (MALD) and MALD-J (Jammer) weapons in the internal weapons bay.[28] Future modifications include the radar modernization program (RMP), which will develop, integrate, test, and replace the unreliable AN/APQ-166 with a modern radar system to enable continued B-52 combat capability with accurate all-weather weapon employment through its extended service life. These and other modifications support ASB and Pacific rebalancing efforts by extending the utility of the B-52 weapon system in A2/AD environments.

Bomber – B-2A Spirit - The B-2 uses low observable (LO) technology to penetrate the world's most sensitive airspace guarded by the most sophisticated defenses. The B-2's LO characteristics result from a combination of reduced infrared, acoustic, electromagnetic, visual, and radar signatures. This combat-proven bomber, from Operations ALLIED FORCE, ENDURING FREEDOM, IRAQI FREEDOM, and ODYSSEY DAWN, can fly long-range strikes to drop large quantities of conventional and nuclear munitions. Its ability to penetrate air defenses and hold any enemy target at risk provides a strong, visible, and effective deterrent and combat force to the CCDRs. To ensure future B-2 weapon system viability in all combat environments, AFGSC is working to complete installation of Defensive Management System Modernization (DMS-M) and secure Beyond-Line-of-Site (BLOS)

---

[27] *Air-Sea Battle.* Air-Sea Battle Office, May 2013, 4.
[28] *B-52 Master Plan.* AFGSC Directorate of Plans, Programs, Requirements, and Assessments, June 2012, 12.

communications. The B-2 Stores Management Processor Rehost will give expanded processing capability and allow full integration of B61 Life Extension Program (LEP) upgrades. Additionally, AFGSC is pursuing a mixed carriage modification to allow the B-2 to carry the Rotary Launcher Assembly (RLA) in one weapons bay and Smart Bomb Rack Assembly (SBRA) in the other weapons bay, thereby increasing B-2 combat capability.[29]

Long Range Strike Bomber (LRS-B) - The LRS-B will be an integral element in the Air Force's future Long Range Strike Family of Systems which will include and integrate intelligence, surveillance and reconnaissance (ISR), electronic attack (EA), and command, control and communications (C^3) assets. It will be nuclear capable when it is fielded in the mid-2020s. Two years after it achieves conventional Initial Operational Capability (IOC), the LRS-B will be nuclear-certified in a separate increment. The LRS-B will provide the Air Force with a future penetrating capability capable of performing both conventional and nuclear deterrent missions in contested airspace against modern integrated air defenses.

Long Range Stand-Off Missile (LRSO) - The AGM-86 Air Launch Cruise Missile (ALCM) has been an integral part of our stand-off nuclear deterrent capability since the early 1980s. Various upgrades and service life extension programs have maintained a viable stand-off missile, but the need for a future stand-off deterrent makes the LRSO essential to modernization. The LRSO program seeks to identify viable concepts and materiel solutions to replace the legacy ALCM in support of deterrence, assurance, and global strike operations. Fielding the LRSO will economically modernize areas of weapon surety, survivability, effectiveness, and reliability.

Gravity Weapons - Today's gravity weapon inventory consists of the B83 and five distinct variants of the B61, each requiring unique and complex logistical support. To simplify the logistics requirements and address aging components on the legacy weapons, the B61 LEP with USAF-provided Tailkit Assembly (TKA) extends the B61's safety, security, and reliability for decades to come.[30] A key component of the Nuclear Weapons Council's "3+2" warhead strategy, the B61-12 enables the reduction of the nuclear stockpile through the consolidation and retirement of legacy gravity weapons while preserving the necessary capabilities to meet our national strategic guidance and US assurance and extended deterrence commitments to NATO. Until the B61-12 achieves full operational capability (FOC), the need to maintain the required number of B83 gravity weapons remains.

ICBM – LGM-30G Minuteman III - The Minuteman ICBM system has been on continuous alert since being first deployed in the 1960's—over 50 years ago. It is the only land-based ICBM operated by the United States and provides a quick-reacting, inertially guided, survivable component to America's strategic deterrent program. Missiles are dispersed in hardened silos to protect against attack and connected to an underground Launch Control Center (LCC) through a system of hardened cables. However, to address its aging components AFGSC is modernizing the Minuteman III to ensure the reliability, survivability, and efficacy of the weapon system through 2030.[31] Minuteman III modernization efforts encompass infrastructure, support equipment, and missile components.[32]

ICBM – Minuteman III Recapitalization - Given that the Minuteman III weapon system and its components have long outlived their originally projected service lives and the increasingly difficult challenges of sustaining legacy systems and integrating new technologies, the time has come to move towards replacing the Minuteman III with a new ground based strategic deterrent capability. AFGSC will continue to define requirements,

[29] *B-2 Master Plan*. AFGSC Directorate of Plans, Programs, Requirements, and Assessments, June 2012, 5-8.

[30] Kehler, Gen C. Robert. "Statement of Commander USSTRATCOM Before the House Committee on Armed Services Subcommittee on Strategic Forces," 29 October 2013, 3-4.

[31] *John Warner National Defense Authorization Act for Fiscal Year 2007, Section 139,* 17 October 2006.

[32] *ICBM Master Plan*. AFGSC Directorate of Plans, Programs, Requirements, and Assessments, December 2013, 8-11.

assess concepts, and identify characteristics required for a Minuteman III follow-on system to ensure a viable ground based strategic deterrent well into the future. Meanwhile, Minuteman III weapon system modernization and the Ground Based Strategic Deterrent (GBSD) analysis of alternatives (AoA) begun in 2013 leverage one another to provide enduring, strategically stabilizing force capability that maximizes synergy and provides future cost savings.[33]

Nuclear Command, Control, and Communications (NC3) - The NC3 infrastructure has supported the strategic nuclear mission for well over 50 years. NC3 includes the emergency action message (EAM) dissemination systems and those systems used for force management, planning, situation monitoring, decision making, and force direction. After 50 years of continuous operation, maintaining these legacy NC3 systems has grown more challenging. As the executive agent responsible for two-thirds of the nation's nuclear triad, AFGSC leadership in NC3 modernization is critical to the deterrence and assurance mission set. Working closely with the US Navy, AFGSC will continue to advocate for the modernization and acquisition to provide a reliable and survivable NC3 network for the President. Nuclear deterrence does not exist without NC3.

Helicopter – UH-1N Iroquois "Huey" - AFGSC operates three UH-1N helicopter squadrons dedicated and committed to providing a flexible and responsive lift capability for nuclear security. ICBM missile fields are located in five northern states (Colorado, Montana, Nebraska, North Dakota, and Wyoming) where winter weather, spring floods, and the remote expanse of the missile complexes drive a multi-faceted security requirement. The UH-1N's primary mission is to provide rapid, flexible, and responsive security force airlift to any location within the missile complex 24/7. The airlift mission ensures Tactical Response Force Emergency Security Responses, daily Missile Security Support during convoy operations, and missile security forward presence operations throughout the AFGSC missile fields. Additionally, these workhorse helicopters provide training platforms to ensure combat mission ready aircrews, integrated aircrew and security forces tactics, techniques, and procedures, as well as transportation support to missile crews and missile maintenance, and finally search and rescue capability.

Helicopter – UH-1N Follow-On - As the UH-1N does not meet DoD survivability, carrying capacity, endurance, or speed requirements, AFGSC is working toward the development and acquisition of a follow-on system which will meet all nuclear security mission requirements, while sustaining the current UH-1N and employing risk mitigation measures to ensure ICBM security.

Air and Space Operations Center (AOC) – 608 AOC – The 608 AOC is designated as USSTRATCOM's Joint Air and Space Operations Center (JAOC) and is a global, functional AOC that plans, executes, and assesses operational-level Assurance, Deterrence, and Global Strike options in response to a full range of global threats to meet CCDR objectives. The 608 AOC is a leading player in emerging Integrated Nuclear Conventional Operations (INCO) development as well as joint standoff munitions planning integration with the origination of the Standoff Munitions Application Center (SMAC). In the realm of BLOS Command and Control (C^2), the 608 AOC created a global B-2 secure communications capability and continues to expand upon existing C^2 technologies by exploring and testing methods to link them together in a worldwide synchronized network in order to best support the CCDR, counter A2/AD challenges, and support the ASB concept. Collectively, these warfighting innovations support USSTRATCOM's priority, *"Partner with the other combatant commands to win today."[34]*

[33] *Air Force 101 Presentation.* AF/CCX, July 2013, slide 51. Website: *https://www.my.af.mil/11421/public/HAF/Air_Force_101_Jul2013.pptx*
[34] *Haney*, CCDR Guidance Memo, 2.

Section 4: Conclusion

This AFGSC SMP supports the objectives of the 2013 Air Force Posture Statement, the 2012 DSG, the 2010 NPR, and the 2014 QDR. In particular, the 2012 DSG underscored the critical importance of the nuclear mission by stating, "As long as nuclear weapons remain in existence, the United States will maintain a safe, secure, and effective arsenal. We will field nuclear forces that can under any circumstances confront an adversary with the prospect of unacceptable damage, both to deter potential adversaries and to assure U.S. allies and other security partners that they can count on America's security commitments."[35]

The AFGSC SMP charts a course for mission accomplishment, while providing flexibility in a dynamic operating environment. Our four priorities focus the actions of our AFGSC Airmen on our mission: *developing and providing combat ready forces for nuclear deterrence and global strike operations...safe, secure, effective...to support the President of the United States and combatant commanders.*

Our vision of an elite, highly disciplined team of Airmen having a special trust and responsibility for the most powerful weapons in our nation's arsenal provides the guidance necessary to establish a values-based culture. Individual responsibility, continual self-assessment, strict adherence to regulations, expertise, pride, respect, safety, resilience, and innovation are this command's foundational values. These values underpin the culture required within the command to shoulder the burden of the nation's highest trust and responsibility.

As we face the challenges of tomorrow, there is much work ahead--but we are up to the challenge. Our nation has placed great trust in this command as the principal steward of our nation's greatest military capabilities; the men and women of AFGSC accept this responsibility with quiet determination. We stand committed to the defense of the United States of America, ready and willing to deter our enemies, assure our allies and partners, and conduct global strike operations--whenever called upon.

---

[35] *2012 DSG*, 5.

Annex A: Acronyms and Abbreviations

A2/AD – anti-access/area denial
AF – Air Force
AFB – Air Force base
AFRC – Air Force Reserve Command
AFGSC – Air Force Global Strike Command
AFSEA – Air Force Strategic Environmental
    Assessment
ALCM – Air-launched cruise missile
ANG – Air National Guard
AoA – Analysis of Alternatives
AOC – Air and Space Operations Center
ASAT - anti-satellite weapon
ASB – Air-Sea Battle Concept
BLOS – Beyond Line of Site
C^2 – Command and Control
C^3 – Command, Control, and Communications
CCDR – combatant commander
CFL – Core Function Lead
C-MAJCOM – Component Major Command
CONECT – Combat Network Communications
    Technology
CBP – Continuous Bomber Presence
CSAF – Chief of Staff, United States Air Force
CSNO – Conventional Support to Nuclear Operations
DMS-M – Defensive Management System
    Modernization
DoD – Department of Defense
DRU – direct reporting unit
DSG – Defense Strategic Guidance
EA – electronic attack
EAM – emergency action message
EHF – extremely high frequency
FOC – full operational capability
GBSD – Ground Based Strategic Deterrent
ICBM – intercontinental ballistic missile
IOC – Initial Operational Capability
IRBM – intermediate range ballistic missile
ISR – Intelligence, Surveillance and Reconnaissance
IWBU – Internal Weapons Bay Upgrade
JASSM – Joint Air-to-Surface Standoff Missile
JASSM-ER – Joint Air-to-Surface Standoff Missile-
    Extended Range
JDAM – Joint Direct Attack Munition
LCC – launch control center
LEP – Life Extension Program
LO – low observable
LRS – long range strike
LRSO – Long Range Stand-Off
MAJCOM – major command
MALD – Miniature Air Launched Decoy

NC3 – nuclear command, control, and
    communications
NMS – National Military Strategy
NPR – Nuclear Posture Review
NDO – Nuclear Deterrence Operations
QDR – Quadrennial Defense Review
RLA – Rotary Launcher Assembly
RMP – Radar Modernization Program
SAM – surface-to-air missile
SecAF – Secretary of the Air Force
SecDef – Secretary of Defense
SBRA – Smart Bomb Rack Assembly
SMP – Strategic Master Plan
TFE – Total Force Enterprise
TKA – Tailkit Assembly
USAF – United States Air Force
USSTRATCOM – United States Strategic Command
WMD – weapon of mass destruction
WSEP – Weapon System Evaluation Program

Annex B: References

Air Force 101 Presentation. AF/CCX, July 2013.
   https://www.my.af.mil/11421/public/HAF/Air_Force_101_Jul2013.pptx

Air Force Priorities Presentation. AF/CCX, June 2013. https://www.my.af.mil/gcss-
   af/USAF/AFP40/d/s6925EC1356510FB5E044080020E329A9/Files/editorial/Air Force Priorities.pdf

Air-Sea Battle. Air-Sea Battle Office, May 2013.

B-2 Master Plan. AFGSC Directorate of Plans, Programs, Requirements, and Assessments, June 2012.

B-52 Master Plan. AFGSC Directorate of Plans, Programs, Requirements, and Assessments, June 2012.

Donley, Michael B., Secretary of the Air Force. Address. AFGSC activation ceremony, Barksdale AFB LA, 7 August
   2009.

Hagel, Chuck, Secretary of Defense. Address. F.E. Warren AFB, 9 January 2014.

Haney, ADM Cecil D. "Combatant Commander's Guidance Memo #1," Headquarters United States Strategic
   Command, 27 November 2013.

ICBM Master Plan. AFGSC Directorate of Plans, Programs, Requirements, and Assessments, December 2013.

John Warner National Defense Authorization Act for Fiscal Year 2007, 17 October 2006.

Kehler, Gen C. Robert. "Statement of Commander USSTRATCOM Before the House Committee on Armed Services
   Subcommittee on Strategic Forces," 29 October 2013.

Kowalski, Lt Gen James M. Critical Days of Summer Memo to AFGSC Personnel, 24 May 2011.

National Military Strategy 2011: February 2011. Department of Defense, 8 February 2011.

Nuclear Posture Review Report: April 2010. Department of Defense, 6 April 2010.

Quadrennial Defense Review Report 2014. Department of Defense, 4 March 2014.

Schwartz, Gen Norton A., Chief of Staff, US Air Force. Address. AFGSC activation ceremony, Barksdale AFB LA,
   7 August 2009.

Sustaining U.S. Global Leadership: Priorities for 21st Century Defense, January 2012. Department of Defense,
   5 January 2012.

USAF Posture Statement: April 2013. Department of the Air Force, April 2013.

USAF Strategic Planning 2010-2030, Strategic Environmental Assessment. Headquarters Air Force, 11 March 2011.

US Census Bureau. "Trade in Goods with Asia" https://www.census.gov/foreign-trade/balance/c0016.html#2013.

Welsh, Gen Mark A., Chief of Staff, US Air Force. Address. Air Force Association Air & Space Conference and
   Technology Exposition, Washington, DC, 18 September 2012.

"To Deter and Assure"